A SUPERHERO YOU

Activate Your Unstoppable Powers

WRITTEN BY BARBARA ANNE COOKSON

WITH KIM SMITH

An Unbelievable Freedom Book

Designed and formatted by Eled Cernik.
ISBN-13: 978-1-7342911-0-0

A Special Message

Before my dad passed away in 2008,
he wrote a letter to all of us. I keep a copy in my desk
and want to share his message with you.

My gift *to* you is something I want *from* each of you. Simply this:

Measure your wealth in the love you give to each other, and the love you receive in return. Give of your true self, and your wealth will be multiplied. If you can give to me what I ask, I will have given you a special gift to cherish, and my wealth will have grown immeasurably.

-Peter Cookson, Superhero Dad

I hope this book grows your wealth immeasurably,
Barb

Table of Contents

A Special Message 3

Welcome from Kim 6

Introduction. 7

How To Use This Book 8

SUPERPOWER #1: ENGAGEMENT
Be Engaged 9

Superpower #1: Engagement 10

Exercise 12

Engagement I.Q.s 14

SUPERPOWER #2: AWARENESS
Be Aware 17

Superpower #2: Awareness 18

Exercise 20

Awareness I.Q.s 22

SUPERPOWER #3: WILLINGNESS
Be Willing 25

Superpower #3: Willingness 26

Exercise 28

Willingness I.Q.s. 30

SUPERPOWER #4: OPENNESS
Be Open 33

Superpower #4: Openness 34

Exercise 38

Openness I.Q.s 40

SUPERPOWER #5: CONFIDENCE
Be Confident 43
Superpower #5: Confidence 44
Exercise 46
Confidence I.Q.s 48

SUPERPOWER #6: KINDNESS
Be Kind 51
Superpower #6: Kindness 52
Exercise 54
Kindness I.Q.s 56

SUPERPOWER #7: BELIEF
Believe 59
Superpower #7: Belief 60
Exercise 64
Belief I.Q.s 66

SUPERPOWER #8: LOVE
Be Love 69
Superpower #8: Love 70
Exercise 72
Love I.Q.s 74

Troubleshooting Questions 76
A Superhero You 78
A Superhero You Checklist 80

Welcome from Kim

Greetings!

Thanks for reading *A Superhero You: Activate Your Unstoppable Powers* by Barbara Anne Cookson. It's the 3rd Unbelievable Freedom Book in the format of a workbook-style Habit Guide. I created the first two on my own, and I enjoyed the process thoroughly. More importantly, readers responded that they appreciated a light, accessible, actionable workbook, so I began to envision collaborating with co-authors on other topics.

Around that same time, I met Barb at the Maine Women's Conference. She was not in her superhero costume, nor did I know the framework she teaches about inner superpowers. She approached my table and we had a conversation about my book *Unmired*, my transformation, and my relationship with my grandmother. The conversation was honest and moving, and I was tearful as we embraced and promised to meet again soon. I don't know if Barb felt subdued that day, or if she was just emitting energy to match mine, but it was a special encounter.

The next time I saw Barb, I was much more attuned to her Superhero vibe. She's ebullient, bubbling over with positive energy and enthusiasm for life. There's an aura of electricity around her. She even drives a "happy car", bright yellow with smiling emojis and a custom vanity plate. It was instantly clear that she not only talks the talk, she walks the walk as she channels her inner superpowers outwardly.

Though I love Barb's high energy, upbeat persona, I asked her to contribute to this series because of the experience on the day we met. Without knowing we might do business together, she gave love out into the world by connecting with me about my grandmother and my story. Gram would have loved Barb, and you will, too.

Enjoy Your Life,
Kim

Introduction

This workbook is meant to be a primer, a starting point on the journey to your inner Superhero.

Being a Superhero means showing up in every single moment the best you can on any given day and coming from a place of love to deliver your unique gifts to the world. That's it. And your best is going to be different every day. Some days, your best is staying in your jammies and napping with the dog. And that's okay.

This book introduces the eight Superpowers that we all come here with, that when activated or turned on, bring us into our full potential. The contents of this book were given to me by my guides. We all have guides who travel through this life with us, offering support, guidance, and unconditional love. Over the years, I have come to appreciate mine as that constant presence and connection to my higher self.

I've known I had this book inside me but was unsure exactly what form it would take. I struggled to get it out of my head and onto the page. It wasn't until I just sat down and asked aloud, "Okay, guides, I know I'm supposed to write this book, just what am I supposed to write?" Instantly, I had it, all wrapped up in the eight powers. My guides have a great sense of humor. I heard them laugh, and they gave me the list. I immediately wrote them down, and like I always do, I questioned them. "Is this it?" Again they laughed. "That's it. Try it. Apply the powers in any situation, and you'll undoubtedly find clarity."

So I did. I've tested these powers in my own life and for years with my coaching clients. In every instance, remembering these powers has helped me, and every one of my clients, to activate our Unstoppable Powers. I've heard others who have received these sorts of messages from their guides call them "downloads." I never quite understood what they meant until I received mine. That's what it's like, an instant download from some crazy, cosmic intelligence with a sense of humor.

I've continued to cultivate a relationship with my guides, and they have become an invaluable source of wisdom, insight, ideas, and, above all, love. If you haven't met yours, ask. They are patiently waiting for your invitation.

How To Use This Book

Maya Angelou said, “you can’t really know where you are going until you know where you have been.” This workbook will help you figure out where you’ve been, where you are now, and what you can do to change the things in your life you want to change.

The Superpowers I describe are powers we all have but have forgotten to use. Each section will introduce a Superpower, then offer questions designed to help you activate that power within you. I’ve also included suggestions for ways to feel that power in your body physically as an exercise.

The questions are meant to make you reflect, to think about how you might change, improve, and grow, better your relationships, your business, your career, or even your health. I call them I.Q.s., Introspective Questions, to guide you on your journey to turning on your Unstoppable Power.

You can use these questions as an inventory of your life. You can go from front to back, building on each, or follow your intuition and go to the ones that speak to you. There’s no wrong way to growth. I’ve even included a list of questions designed to help you to deal with specific situations where you may be feeling stuck, a sort of troubleshooting guide. I added pages for your ideas, thoughts, notes, and plans. Use this space for what I call brain dumping. Just dump our whatever comes to mind.

I’ve used these questions for myself in all situations, and they’ve helped me find clarity and peace when making big decisions. Now my clients and my audiences have used them as well. Remembering these Unstoppable Powers will change your life. You are about to meet A Superhero You.

I’ve used these questions for myself in all situations, and they’ve helped me find clarity and peace when making big decisions. Now my clients and audiences have used them as well. Remembering these Unstoppable Powers will change your life. You are about to meet A Superhero You.

SUPERPOWER #1: ENGAGEMENT

Be Engaged

Show up in every single moment like you are supposed to be there.

MARIE FORLEO

Superpower #1: Engagement

I'll never forget Sister Elizabeth in my freshman Algebra 1 class in high school. On this particular sunny day, I was less interested in learning formulas than in watching the traffic going by three stories down out the middle pane of the window of the back of the class. Sister Elizabeth was standing at the chalkboard in her starched black habit. She was barely 5'2", but she was a force. She was reading the roll call. I heard my name, and without turning to see her, poised, arm stretched back like a major league pitcher, shouted, "here." Suddenly, SMASH! A large piece of white chalk shattered on the window just past my nose. I turned back around with an audible gasp to see Sister Elizabeth grinning a sinister grin from the front of the room. "You say you are present, but you are not engaged, Miss Cookson."

What is Engagement? Engagement is an active presence. How many days do we flow through not being actively engaged in the moments as they happen around us? How many of us have driven the interstate past our exit, only to notice we've gone too far? Or walked into a room and forgotten why we were there in the first place? We even hear stories in the news about people who've forgotten children in a hot car for so many hours they die from inattention. How is this possible? It's disengagement. We are so scattered and stressed and spread so thin trying to keep up, that we can't possibly focus on the present moments in our lives. We are trying to do everything and accomplishing nothing.

We have no focus. We're driving around in these amazing, miraculous bodies as a completely distracted driver. Our minds are in constant discussion with us about anything and everything, trivial and essential, dissolving our focus from what is the only important thing right now: right now. When I yelled "here" to Sister Elizabeth, you could argue that I was present—but was I engaged? Not really. We can think of Engagement as being grounded. It is our foundational power. Being engaged and grounded in our physical body and, metaphorically, to our source power, as well as to each other, allows us to grow our inner Superhero.

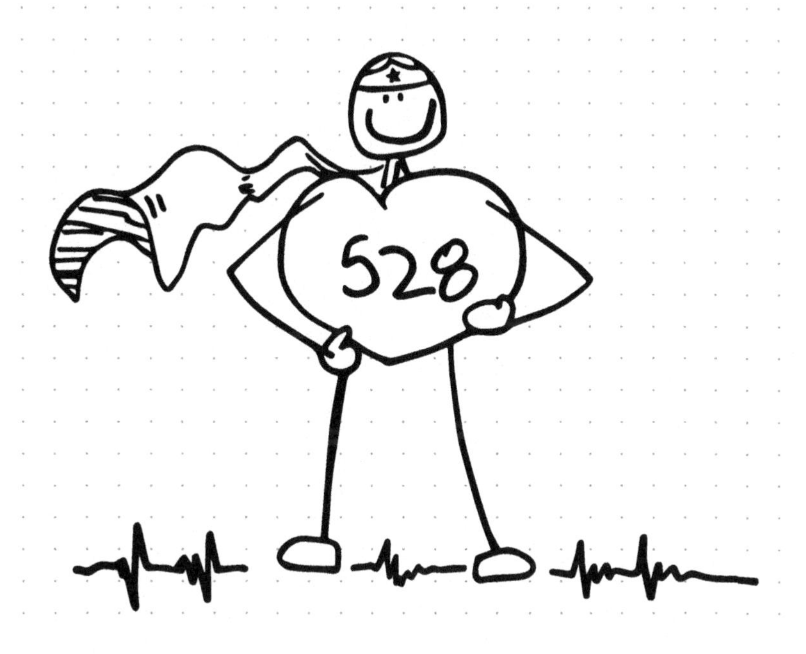
528

Exercise

I promised a suggestion for a physical movement to start to activate this power in your body. For Engagement, we're going to engage your core. If you've ever had a personal trainer or taken a group fitness class, you've undoubtedly heard your instructor shout, "Engage your core!" I teach group fitness, and I say this all the time. It's a perfect way to remember to be engaged in the moment. When I ask you to engage your core, I don't mean to suck in your gut. Most people draw in a huge breath, suck in their tummy, and hold it. That's NOT engaging your core.

Engaging your core means tightening and tensing the muscles in your trunk and abs as if preparing for someone to punch you in the belly. You also engage the pelvic floor muscles (those muscles you squeeze when trying not to pee). It's a perfect example of strength and power and brings you into the now in a big way.

This movement can be practiced anywhere, anytime, and will bring you into the present moment where you are. You'll come into your physical body in a way that awakens your energy system, as well. Ultimately, the purpose of this movement is to feel your body and to move energy. Engaging the muscles of your core not only gives you great abs, but it also helps to move that energy up to your brain, in turn raising your brainwave frequencies. Think of it like squeezing a freezer pop to get the popsicle up the tube. We are moving energy from a lower, stagnated form of energy to a higher, lighter, healthier frequency.

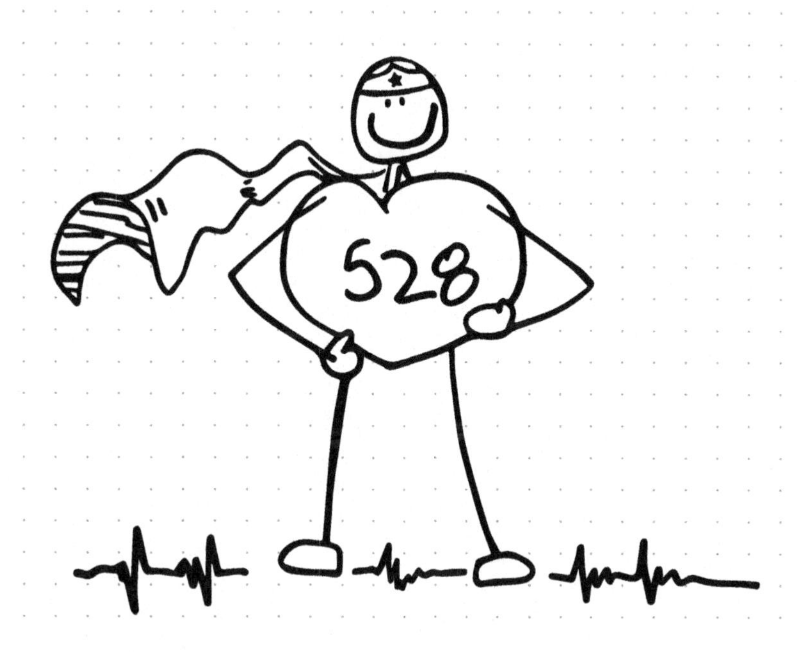
528

Engagement I.Q.s

How have I been disengaged in my life?

With my family?

With my health?

Where do I need to put my focus today to allow me to move forward?

What will I do to engage more fully today?

In my work?

In my relationships?

In my body?

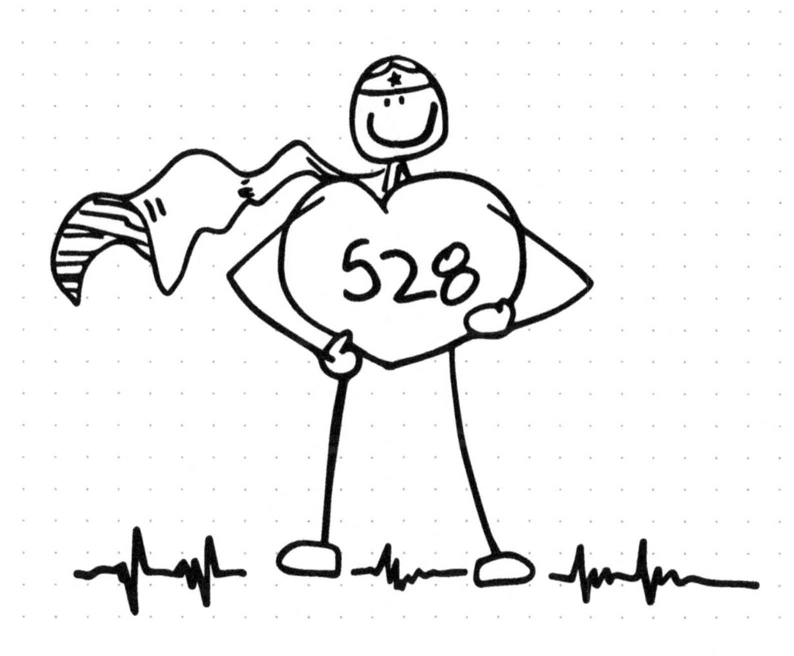
528

SUPERPOWER #2: AWARENESS

Be Aware

Everything is energy,
and that's all there is to it.

ALBERT EINSTEIN

Superpower #2: Awareness

Awareness is a HUGE topic, but for our purposes, there are three foundational Awarenesses we need to have to activate our Unstoppable Power. The first is energy. Energy is a deep subject, but for now, here are the basics. We must be aware that we are energy. Every atom, every cell, every tissue, every organ, every thought in our body and mind is made up of energy. That energy moves around us and through us and out to the world. Energy is palpable. We all know someone that we don't want to be around. You know the ones, the negative Nellies and angry Andy's. The minute they walk in the room, you feel the energy sucked out of you. That's their energy you're feeling. Don't be that person. Be aware of your energy and what you are sharing with the world. Be the energy you want to attract.

The second Awareness is language. We all have an internal dialogue, a negative language that I call your backseat driver, or BSD. It's that little voice in your head that is continually chatting away at you, and usually, it's giving you grief. It's that voice that says, "What do you think you're doing? Who do you think you are? You shouldn't be doing this. You shouldn't wear that. You shoulda, coulda, woulda, and what are you thinking with that blue eyeshadow?" UGH. This negative language will destroy your inner Superhero. People will tell you that you can quiet those voices and stop the negative self-talk with techniques like breathwork, meditation, biofeedback, I say hooey. You WILL NOT QUIET THEM. Thinking you can only creates more stress. But being aware they are there, and that they are not you, is the first step in dealing with them. Language has power. What we say and what we think carries energy. Thoughts become things. Be aware of the energy your words carry. We'll talk more about your BSD later.

The third Awareness is choice. Between every action and reaction, event and result, question and answer, is a space in time. Sometimes it's short, sometimes longer. But always, always in that space is your power of choice. You have a choice of how to respond, react, or answer. Ultimately, you are who you choose to be. Know that power, use that power, and activate your inner Superhero. If you ever hear yourself saying, I don't have a choice, STOP! Remember this Superpower. Making choices is sometimes just hard. Think outside the box. If you're stuck, ask someone else to look at your situation. Many times, others can give us immediate insight that we don't see. I do this all the time. I have friends that are only a text away that I reach out to regularly on this one. I also believe in a higher power that guides me, and when I'm struggling, I call on my higher power and ask. Identify those people and guides in your life that you can count on for help. The power of choice is our own, but true Superheroes recognize their vulnerabilities and ask for help when they need it.

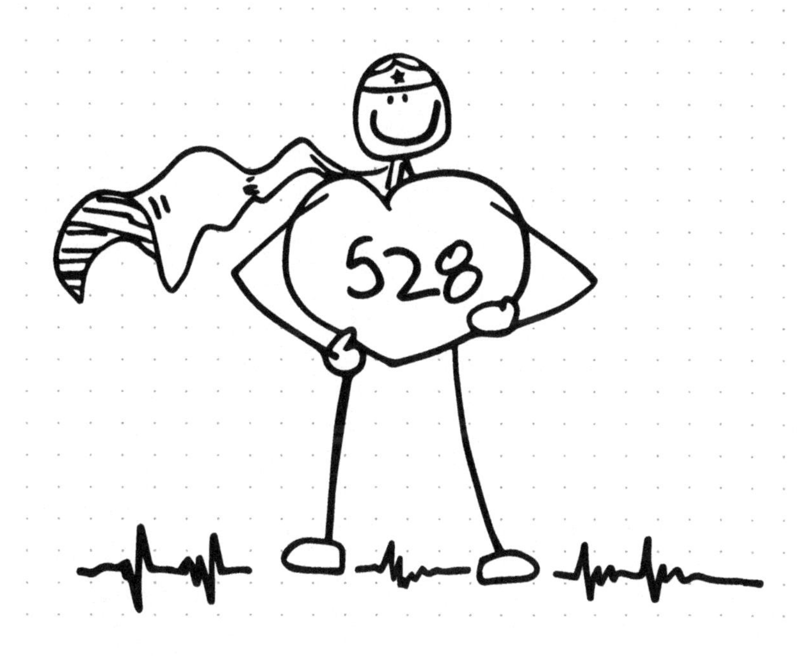
528

Exercise

The movement I associate with the power of Awareness is what I call the Awareness Squat. It's an exercise that will make you aware of your body, bring you into the present, start to activate energy, and give you a great butt! It is a simple (and necessary) exercise to build into your day. You can do it at work, and I suggest setting a reminder, a timer, or putting a sticky note on your calendar or computer screen as a visual reminder to get up and squat.

To do the Awareness Squat, sit ahead slightly on your chair and sit up very straight. Hold your tongue on your palate (this is an energy connection point). With no hands, bring your awareness to the bottom of your feet. Without assistance or pushing yourself up with your hands, press your feet into the floor and use your big muscle groups, your glutes, and your legs to come to standing. The key is to move S-L-O-W-L-Y!

Move through gravity ever so slowly with an engaged core and strong legs. Move around, walk around your desk, take a little break. Then, when you're ready to sit again, do it the same way, no hands, and VERY S-L-O-W-L-Y! This movement can become a habit. Whenever you need to leave your desk or station for any reason, remember to add in the Awareness Squat. At the end of the day, you've done a dozen or so, and will be on your way to a strong, lean lower body. Remember our analogy of the freezer pop? The core is engaged, you are grounded, your energy activated, and with the Awareness Squat, you are continuing to draw energy up into your body. You will be priming your power system, and you will be aware of your quads tomorrow, I guarantee it!

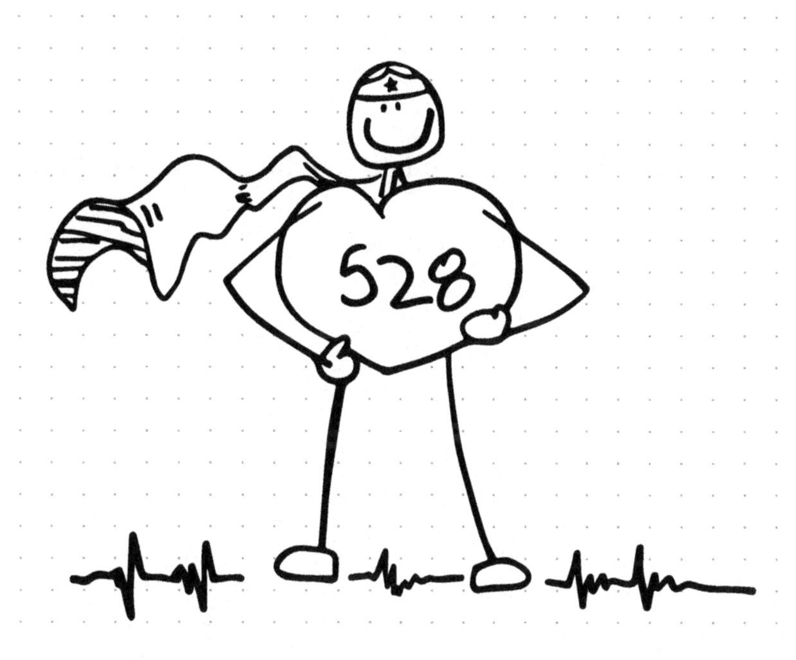
528

Awareness I.Q.s

What is the energy I'm noticing today? (sensing, breathing, seeing, hearing, feeling?)

What is the emotion or mood that I purposefully choose today? (Remember, you don't always have to feel happy. We have a full range of emotions we can feel. If you are feeling sad, that's totally ok. Own it. The idea is to know it's a choice and it's ok.) *See A Superhero You Checklist

How does this energy serve me today? (What is my reward?)

What have my BSDs (back seat drivers) been saying that I need to acknowledge? (If you've had any negative self talk, what is it?)

What will I do today to improve my self talk? (i.e. what will I do to re-focus? To quiet the negative thoughts? Take a walk? Listen to music? What are your specific tools?

What and where are my choices today? What will I intentionally choose?

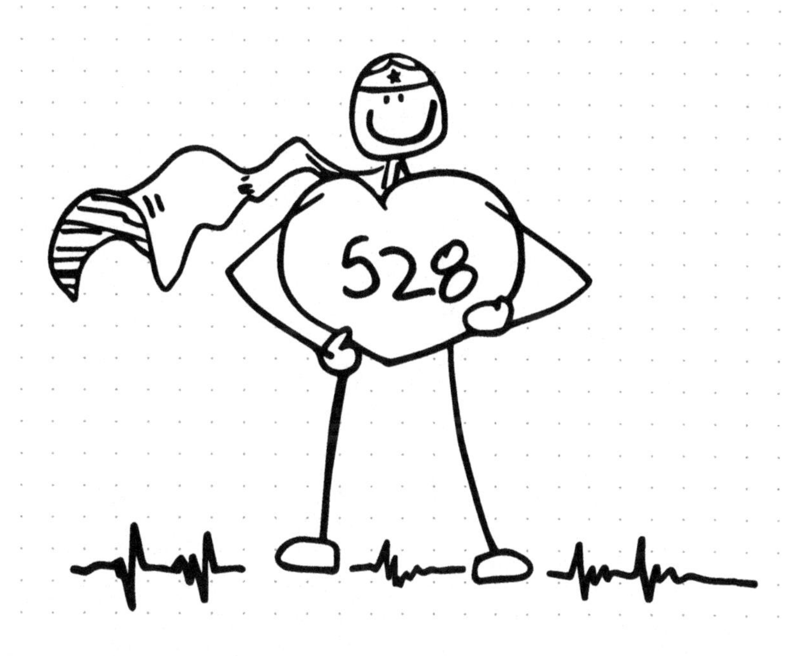
528

SUPERPOWER #3: WILLINGNESS

Be Willing

If you want the things in your life to change, you must be willing to change the things in your life.

UNKNOWN

Superpower #3: Willingness

By definition, willingness is a frame of mind where we choose to let go of fear and let go of fear-based excuses for not changing something for the better. What are some fear-based excuses you have for not being willing to do something? I don't know what might happen; I'm not good enough, I'm too old, too young, too short, too tall, too fat, too thin, too busy—that's the BSD talking. And what do we know about the BSD? It isn't you. Willingness requires Engagement and Awareness of choice. Willingness is anti-avoidance. It's flexible and adaptable. Feel the fear and do it anyway. That's Willingness.

Be willing to let go of what you think you know. Be willing to learn, listen, adapt, be teachable, and to change. As a true Superhero, you must be willing to release the fear and step into your power. Be willing to choose. Be willing to change what needs to be changed to make your life what you want it to be. You own the power, and you need to be willing to express it. Some of us have a hard time with willingness. Willingness takes courage. As we work through these together, you'll start seeing how the Superpowers build on each other. We must first be aware of our power of choice, then be willing to make them.

A potential client came to see me about coaching her. She talked to me about all of the things in her life that she wanted to change. One of them was her weight. She had gained a significant amount of weight and didn't like herself this way. Within a few minutes, she was in tears. During our consultation visit, she adamantly stated she was not willing to give up her pizza and her wine. Period. Do you think she'll lose the weight? Not until she can activate her power of willingness, engagement, awareness, and the rest of the powers you are relearning here.

For some of my clients, it's easier to think of it in another way. Try this. Ask yourself what it is you are NOT willing to do in your life. Identify those things you've been allowing that you know are not serving you. For example, are you allowing someone to mistreat you? Or take advantage of you? Are you staying in a dead-end job just for the paycheck even though it makes you stressed, angry, and unhappy? Are you willing to give up pizza and wine to get healthy? Sometimes, it's easier to say no to those wrong things than to be willing to say yes to the right things. In the end, it's semantics. Both will lead you to your inner Superhero.

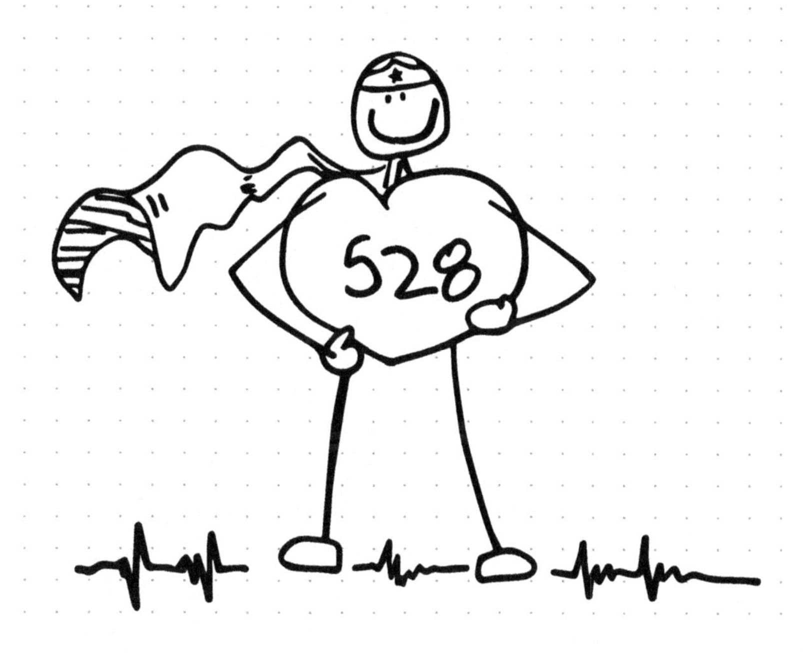
528

Exercise

The movements I encourage you to practice for remembering to be willing are flexibility exercises in the form of neck stretches. These stretches are so beneficial for anyone who works at a desk job, or stands, sits, or works long hours driving. Pretty much all of us. You can do these at work, in the grocery line, in the bathroom, in the car. All of these eight Superpower exercises can be performed anywhere and anytime.

For the flexibility Willingness neck stretches, keep your spine straight, and imagine lifting your ears towards the sky and your shoulders to the earth. Doing this will give you a long, open neck. Place your tongue on your palate, as this connects the energy channels in your body. Take a deep breath in and on the exhale, gently turn your head to look over your right shoulder. On the next inhale, turn your head back to the center. On the exhale, turn your head to look over your left shoulder. On the next inhale, turn your head back to the center. You've now done one round. Continue to complete three to four rounds.

This exercise helps to restore your natural range of motion and increases flexibility.

Next, with ears to the sky and shoulders to the earth, breathe in and slowly stretch your left ear to your left shoulder as far as is comfortable, allowing a gentle stretch. Hold that stretch for fifteen to thirty seconds. Come back to the center, take a breath, and repeat on the other side.

Lastly, again, with your ears to the sky and shoulders to the earth to open the neck, take a deep breath in and slowly stretch your chin to your chest, maintaining a long neck. This stretch feels great and will stretch the muscles down into your shoulders and upper back. Visually, when doing these neck movements, what do you see? It's the movement of nodding "yes" and shaking your head "no." Answering the question: Are you willing?

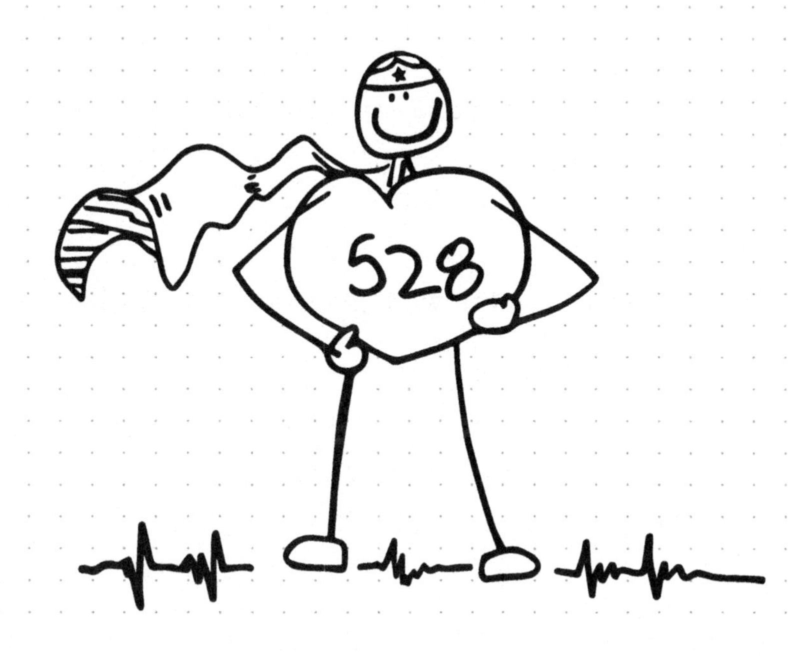
528

Willingness I.Q.s

What am I willing to let go of today that has been holding me back?

What am I willing to change to make my life what I want it to be?

In my relationships?

In my work?

For my health? *See A Superhero You Checklist

Sometimes we can understand the power of Willingness more clearly if we consider what we are UNwilling to allow, be, or do.

What am I unwilling to allow in my life that hinders my progress?

Which behaviors am I unwilling to continue that have inhibited my growth?

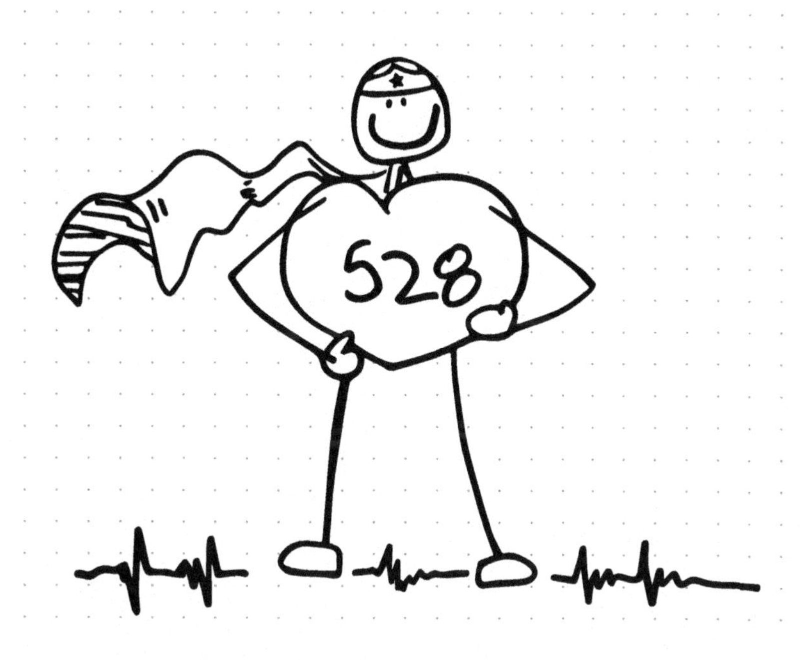
528

SUPERPOWER #4: OPENNESS

Be Open

Be open to any and all possibilities and the signs and synchronicities that lead you to them.

BARBARA ANNE COOKSON

Superpower #4: Openness

This power is about giving and receiving. Be open to receiving all that life has to offer. Be open to accepting. Be open to allowing. Allowing our lives to unfold and knowing that everything will happen right on time. I have a quote by Asha Tyson under the glass surface on top of my desk that reads: "Your journey has molded you for your greater good, and it was exactly what it needed to be. Don't think you've lost time. It took each and every situation you have encountered to bring you to the now. And now is right on time." Be open to experiencing even challenges and difficulties as opportunities. Ralph Marston, founder of The Daily Motivator online, says, "Being open means letting go. Let go of your attachment to being right, and suddenly your mind is more open."

We sometimes need to let go of old ideas and paradigms that keep us where we are instead of where we want to go. Our insecurities hold us back. Instead of allowing great things into our lives, our BSDs try to remind us that we aren't meant to be great, but that greatness is for someone else. We admire and look up to those people we view as Superheroes without ever realizing we are them. We are all the same. Be open to your uniqueness. Embrace it. Be willing to open yourself up to the possibilities that open themselves to you every day.

There are signs all around us that we are where we're supposed to be. Be open to them. I have them all the time. A special song comes on the radio when I'm thinking of a certain person. Or I run into a person I haven't seen in years just when I'm thinking of them. Being open and recognizing these signs in your own life is the key. Are coincidences real? I believe there are no coincidences. Sometimes, an event is like a little slap to the side of your head, saying, "Hey! Pay attention! You're here!" You are where you're supposed to be, and things are right on time.

When my dad passed, my mom kept his dog. This dog was unique and was my dad's companion. When Cooper was seventeen, and it became apparent that we would have to put him down, it was a big deal. My brother, sister, and I went to my mom's house, and we all talked to her about what was best for him. It was an awful decision to make, as any pet owner knows. It was even harder because my mom felt that it was her last connection to my dad (my brother pointed out that, of course, was us). But when it's time, we always question, am I doing the right thing? Is it time? We decided to call and have our vet come to the house and put Cooper down at home. We scheduled for the next day, so we would all be there with him.

That morning, as I was rushing around to get out the door, my dogs started barking like crazy. I went to the door, and standing on my porch was a little dog. Now, my house sits four hundred feet off the road, and there are very few neighbors nearby, and I had never seen this little guy before. I called him and he came over to me, scared and shaking. It was winter, and it was cold. I picked him up and brought him into my office, away from my dogs, and gave him a drink. Now I was running late, and I've got this little dog, my dogs are going nuts, and I had to leave. I had an idea. I went to Facebook, posted a photo of this little guy, and asked if anyone knew where he belonged. Within minutes, I had a hit. My neighbor knew the family and would let them know.

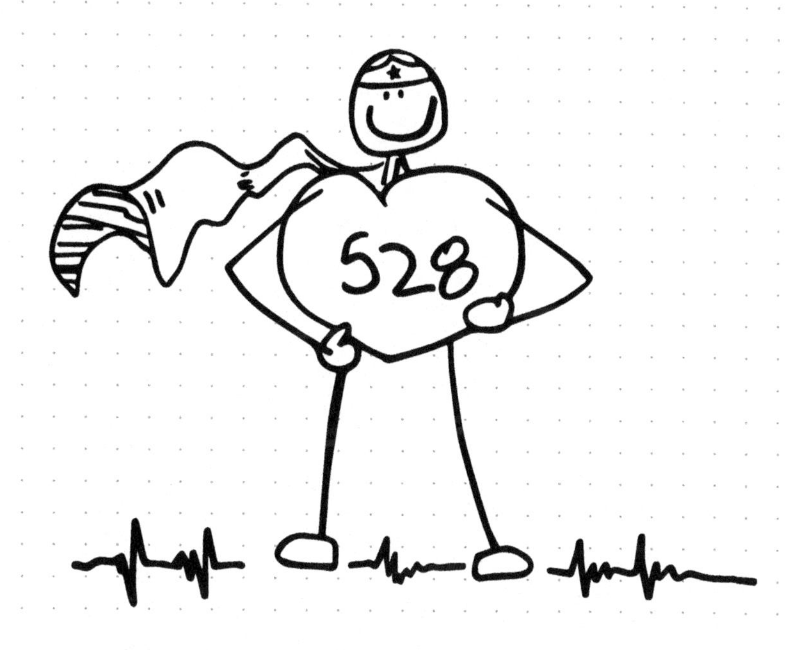
528

A few minutes later, a man and his little boy came to get the pup. I explained how he came onto the porch and came right to me and came in. The man was surprised because he was deaf and very rarely goes to strangers. I asked what his name was, and the man said, “His name is Pete.” I stopped in my tracks. My dad’s name was Pete, and he was deaf. Coincidence? I don’t think so. I was frantically struggling with the imminent death of my dad’s beloved dog, and a deaf stray dog named Pete shows up on my step as I’m going out the door to have my dad’s dog put down. Was it a sign that we were doing the right thing? No. I don’t believe they are signs that we’re making a right or wrong decision. That is our free will (our third power). But I do think that signs are there to send us a clear and important message: you are where you’re supposed to be, and things are right on time.

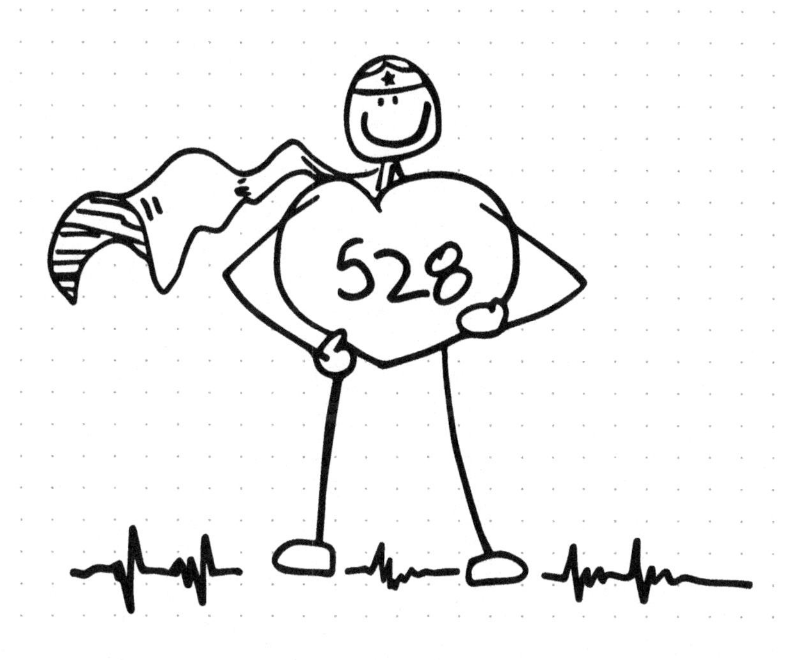
528

Exercise

The movement for remembering to be open is, of course, breath. We learn to breathe shallowly from our upper chest. We're holding in our tummies and stifling our breath. When I ask audiences to take a deep breath in, invariably, I see everyone's shoulders creep up to meet their ears. That is not a deep breath! We need to relearn to breathe fully into our bellies, drawing breath deep into our center and filling up to our collar bones and throat, and then releasing the breath out, filling and emptying.

A great way to practice is to lie on your back with a piece of paper on your tummy. As you breathe in through your nose, feel your belly fill, and see the paper flutter up. As you breathe out, through your mouth, the paper will softly lower. Another powerful exercise is box breathing. This type of breath means that you count your inspirations and the space between them. For example, inhale for a count of four, hold for a count of four, exhale for a count of four, and hold for four. That's one cycle. This one simple but essential exercise instantly reactivates your first four Superpowers. You become grounded, engaged, aware of your body and energy, willing to slow down, and open to possibility. Practice this breath whenever you are feeling stressed, confused, or low on energy. It's always with you, and it's free.

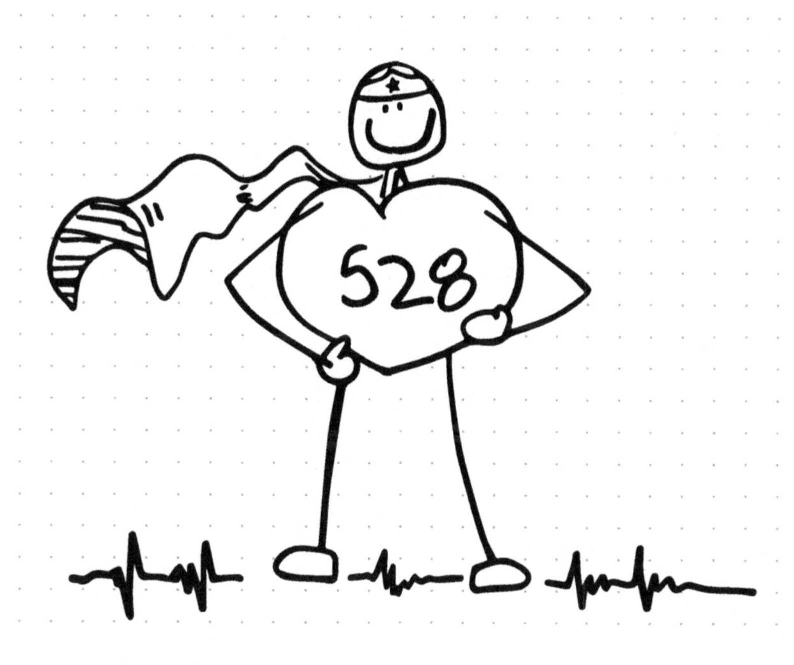
528

Openness I.Q.s

How have I kept myself closed off from others?

How can I be more open to joy in my life today?

Is there someone in my life that needs to be heard? How will I open to just listening without interjecting my thoughts? (Being open is about accepting.)

What opportunities are available to me that I will open myself up to today?

Are there signs that I haven't noticed until now that are showing me I'm where I'm supposed to be? Y / N What are they?

How will I be more open in my breath today? (What 'play" activities can I engage in today to feel more open?)

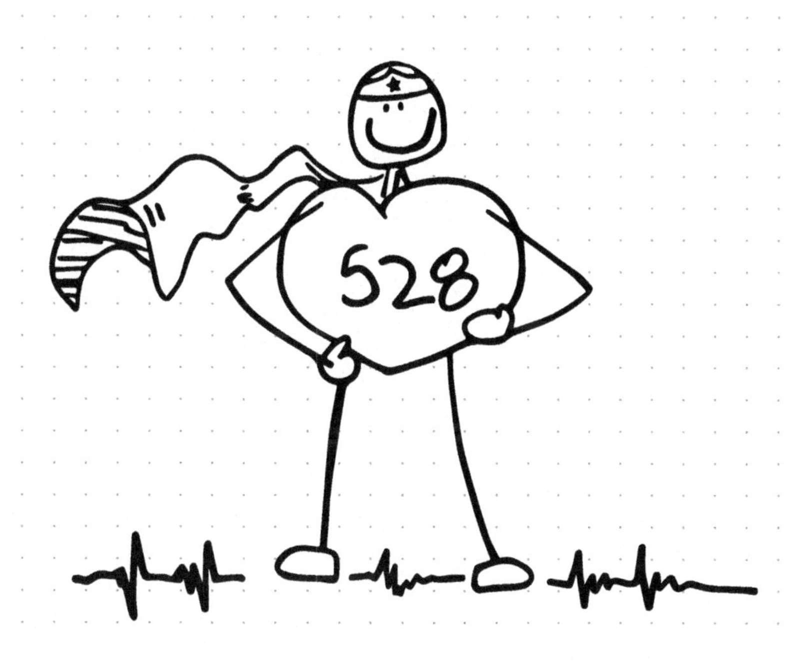
528

SUPERPOWER #5: CONFIDENCE

Be Confident

Confidence is going after Moby Dick in a rowboat and taking tartar sauce with you.

ZIG ZIGLAR

Superpower #5: Confidence

I love that quote. It says that you will succeed. You will never meet a Superhero that doesn't exhibit confidence. Confidence is key. Yet so many of us struggle with this one power. We feel inadequate and less than enough. We compare ourselves to others and tell ourselves we fall short. Why? We lose confidence and self-esteem due to our self-perceived "failures." If we believe we have failed at something, it chips away at our self-confidence. The key is to change our perception of failure. Failure to a confident person doesn't exist. Failure is just experience. It's an experience to be viewed as learning. When we can accept and allow failures to become lessons, we can grow and keep our confidence intact.

When I was little, I used to love to write poems and make words rhyme. I remember it was just joyful. One day, I wrote a silly little poem—I don't recall what it was about—but I was so proud of it. I ran to the kitchen where my mother and my aunt were doing dishes. I excitedly read my poem for them. My aunt turned and laughed. She was making fun of me. She said, "Don't quit your day job." I didn't fully understand the words then, but I understood the meaning. She thought my poem sucked, and I had no talent. I stopped writing poems. I felt ashamed and defeated. I completely lost my confidence. It was years before I wrote again. As children, we begin life with all of these innate Superhero powers that allow us to become what we're meant to be. But through programming from the people who raise us, our environment, and societal expectations, these powers are sometimes forgotten. It's never too late to remember your confidence.

Years ago, I was speaking to a group of college students about success, and we were discussing confidence. One young woman raised her hand and asked, "If I don't have confidence, how can I be confident?" Ahhhh, there's the big question. And here's the answer: Fake it. Fake it 'til you make it. PRETEND! Seriously, act like it! Act, feel, think, be, and do, like a confident Superhero, and you'll be one. Say, I AM! It sounds simplistic, but honestly, that's it. It's what I did. Sweating, and trembling, and dizzy, I learned to fake it. We get good at what we practice. Practice faking it, and it will come.

We all have something we're good at doing. Maybe you are an expert knitter or a speed reader, or you have a gift for baking. You have confidence in those areas. That is proof that you have confidence. You just aren't allowing that confidence to be apparent in other areas of your life. It's there, let it out. Adopt the mindset of a confident person. Think of someone you know who you admire for their confidence. When you're struggling with your confidence, ask yourself how they would handle this. Then do that! Soon, with practice, you can grow your confidence muscles to be strong and healthy.

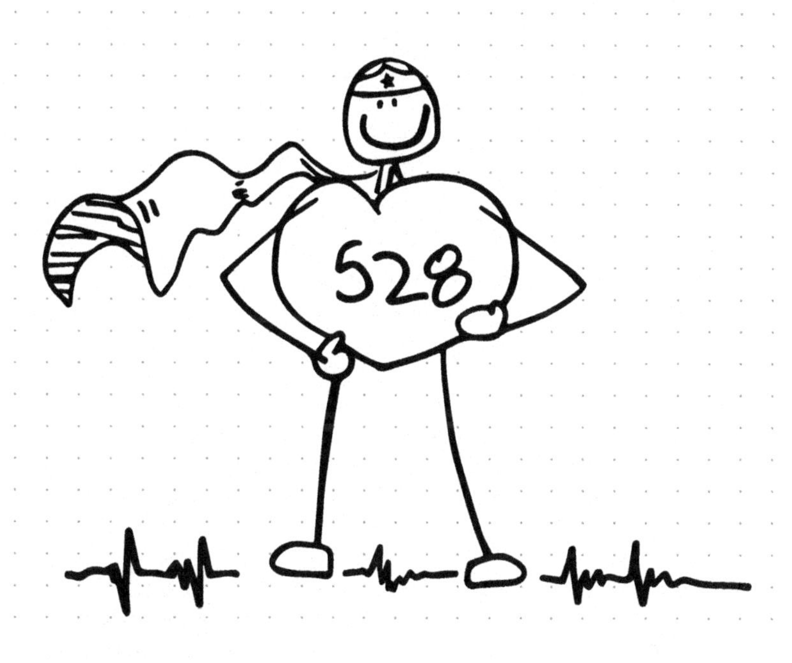
528

Exercise

Confidence exhibits when we open up physically. A physical movement to practice building your confidence muscles is power posing. In a study conducted at Columbia University by researcher and author Amy Cuddy, the research found that by holding one of five demonstrated "power poses" for two minutes, subjects' testosterone levels increased by 20%, and their cortisol levels decreased by 25%. Power posing led to hormonal changes in the body that led to an increased feeling of confidence. Some researchers have questioned her conclusions, but I've practiced this myself when I'm getting ready to speak to audiences, and seen it work for my clients.

So, from now on, when you're facing a situation where you may be questioning your ability, put on that invisible headband, tiara, or cape, take two minutes, and hold that Wonder Woman pose! Practice pretending to be that Superhero you and, soon, she (or he) will appear!

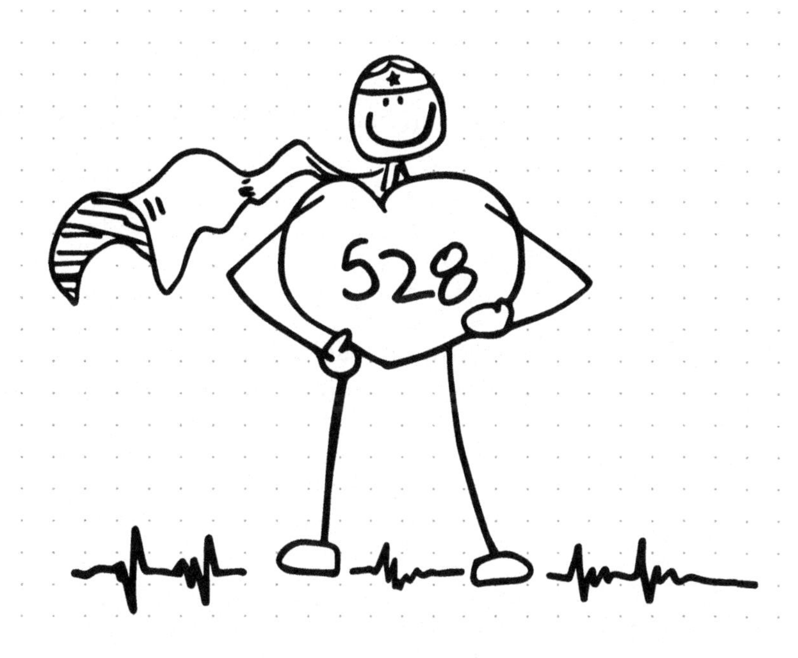
528

Confidence I.Q.s

Do I have a fear of failure? Y / N Why?

In what situations in my life have I failed to exhibit confidence? (what particular instances or experiences come to mind?)

Where did my lack of confidence come from?

How could I have performed differently?

What can I do specifically to empower myself and increase my confidence quotient? (for example: go to a social or networking event, ask a friend for support, join a group or club where you can practice confidence building, etc.)

Am I happy in/with my own body? Y / N If NO, what will I do today to start feeling better? Hint: it's all about the feels.

What will I incorporate into my schedule weekly for a mindful movement practice? (The dreaded exercise question! Be honest and commit. It is crucial for your confidence.)

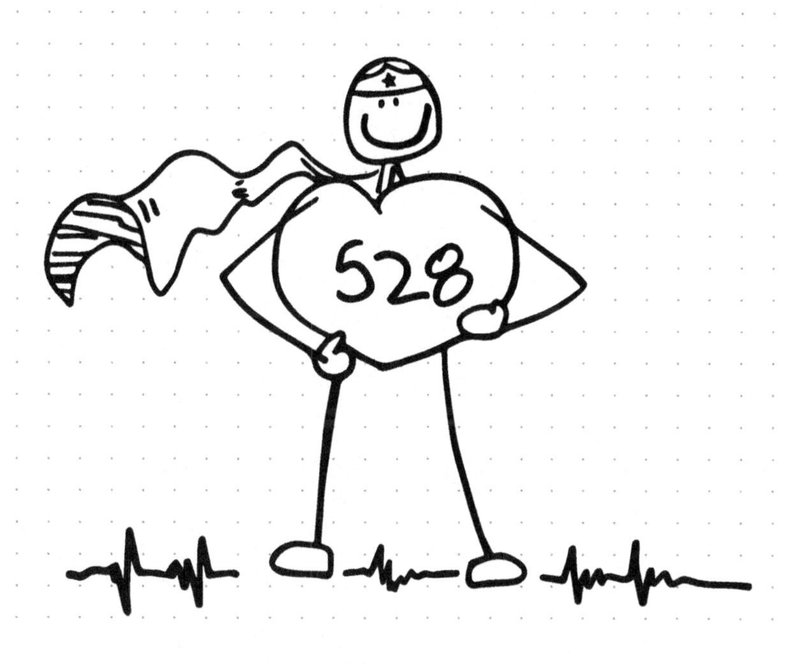
528

SUPERPOWER #6: KINDNESS

Be Kind

Be kind whenever possible. And it is always possible.

THE DALAI LAMA

Superpower #6: Kindness

It's always possible. Remember that Superhero power of choice? Choose to be kind. It's a basic tenet for every organized religion. Look, there are times when all of us are unkind. I'm guilty of it myself. I remember times in my life when I've been unkind to someone, and I still feel remorse today. In particular, a nurse that was assigned to take care of my dad during one of his hospitalizations wasn't very nice. She was rough and didn't seem very compassionate at all. Even after we explained to her that my dad's skin was sensitive and thin, she ripped a bandage from his arm, tearing the skin off with it. It took weeks to heal. We called her "the troll." My Superhero dad reminded us that we never know what someone else is going through. What was she dealing with that made her angry and uncaring? I had never thought about it.

We get mad, frustrated, tired, and we say things we don't mean and do things we wish we hadn't. It's undoubtedly only human. Recognize your humanity, and recognize the humanity in others. Choose to be kind in all situations. When I was a kid, every afternoon after school, I watched Mr. Rogers' Neighborhood on T.V. Mr.Rogers said, "There are three ways to ultimate success: The first way is to be kind. The second way is to be kind. The third way is to be kind."

Kindness begets kindness. Kindness can transform our enemies into friends. Bitterness only hurts the person feeling it. Treat others as you would like them to treat you. And treat YOURSELF with kindness.

Arguably, altruism is a trait of all Superheroes, but being kind to oneself is necessary to activate your Unstoppable Power. Sometimes, we are people pleasers and try to say yes to everyone and everything in an attempt to be all things to all people with the idea that we can't say no and feel good about it. That's not being kind to anyone. If you are one of those people, how does that make you feel? Are you exhausted, drained, empty, resentful?

Years ago, in my massage therapy practice, there was a woman in the waiting area of the office as another client was leaving. The woman going asked me to come to her place of business and do chair massages for an event she was holding after hours (I had done this for her on several occasions). I thanked her for thinking of me but explained that I couldn't do her event and would refer her to a few colleagues available to help. She gladly took the names and went. The woman waiting in the office overheard this conversation and was almost in tears. Her mouth was agape, and she said, "You said NO so easily! I could never do that!" I pointed out to her that saying yes to that would have put a lot of stress on me. It wasn't something that would serve her or me, as I would be exhausted and not perform to her expectations. It would also take away energy from other projects that were more important to me. She understood and said that from that point on, she would be more willing to say NO to the things in her life that didn't serve her. Again, we see the interdependence of our Superpowers: Kindness requires Awareness, Willingness, and Confidence.

528

Exercise

Up until now, I've given you a movement to associate with each power. For this power, it is essential to choose a movement practice for yourself. Be kind to yourself by incorporating a movement practice into your day that you enjoy. Do something every day that makes you feel good, healthy, strong, and happy. It may be just walking your dog. It may be yoga or running or taking a group fitness class. Make intentional movement a part of your routine every day for your own greater good. Your body and your mind will thank you and, ultimately, you will be better prepared to bring your inner Superhero to the world. When you work your kindness muscles in this way towards yourself, they are strengthened to better serve others.

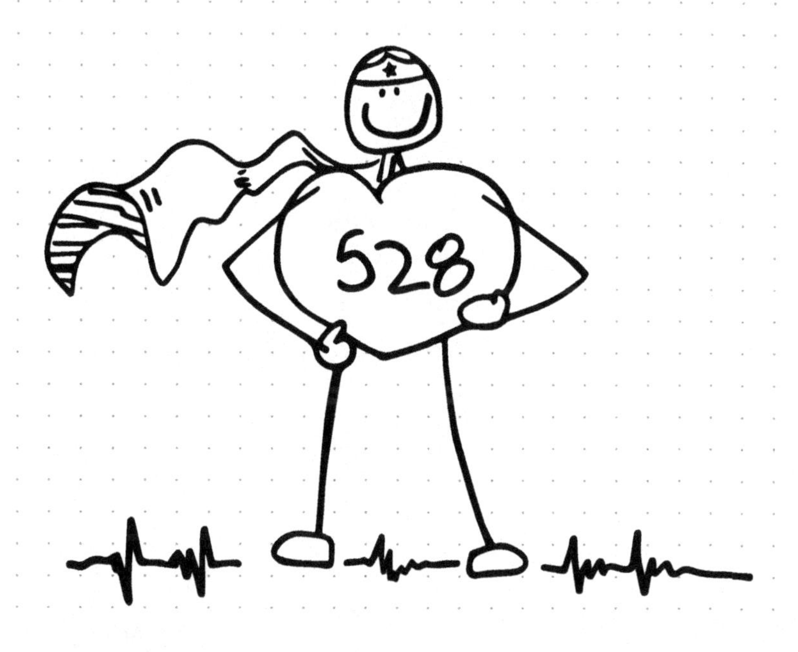
528

Kindness I.Q.s

Am I kind to myself? Y / N What will I do today to show kindness to myself?

How does it make me feel when I'm kind to myself? (is it a good feeling or guilt?)

Am I kind to others? Y / N Who can I be kind to today?

What will I do for someone I know today, for no reward, to make their day better?

Once that's done, how did it make me feel?

What will I do today to be kind to a stranger? (pay for someone's coffee at the drive thru, leave an extra large tip to a deserving server, leave a flower on a windshield?)

Once that's done, how did it make me feel?

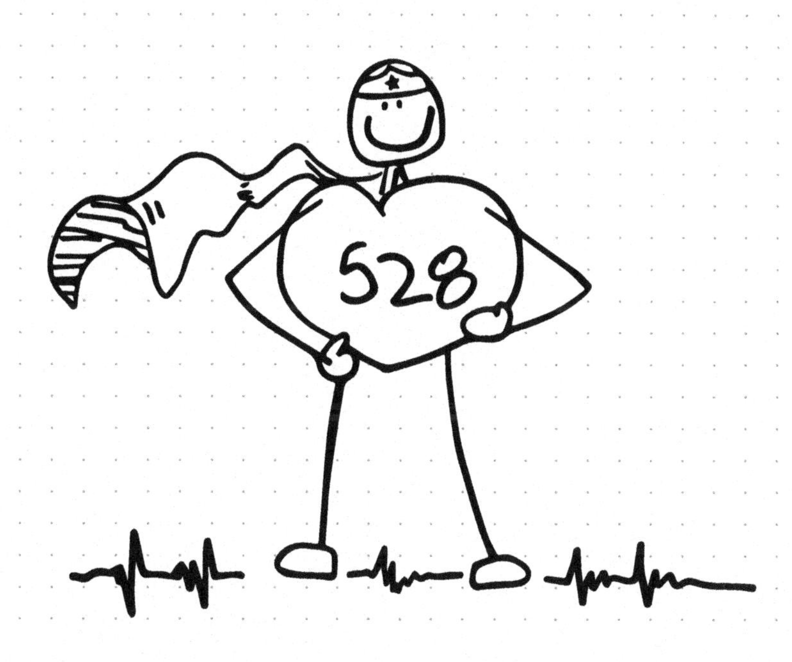
528

SUPERPOWER #7: BELIEF

Believe

Things are only impossible until they are not.

CAPTAIN JEAN LUC PICARD,
STARSHIP ENTERPRISE

Superpower #7: Belief

To be your Superhero self, you need a sense of love and belonging. It's the driving force of every human, wanting to be loved and to belong. Researcher and author Brené Brown said there is only one difference between people with a strong sense of love and belonging and those without a strong sense of love and belonging. It's a belief that they are worthy of love and belonging, A BELIEF. Believe that you are enough. Believe that you are enough just as you are where you are. Your Superhero is activated when you can love yourself, believe in yourself, be kind to yourself, allow yourself the luxury of letting go of expectations, and be who you are. We can strive for mastery over mediocrity, but accepting ourselves as we are is the secret to finding success. Letting go of the disappointment, fear, and anxiety that comes with the imagined notion that you are not enough is what allows your inner Superhero to emerge.

What we choose to believe about ourselves and our circumstances defines who we are. But how do we adopt our beliefs? Can you determine what your beliefs are and where you learned them? We acquire our belief systems from our adult teachers, such as our parents, guardians, and relatives, when we are children. As we grow, we forget where we learned those behaviors, so we accept them as who we are. I challenge you to question what you believe and who taught you.

Do you remember Superpower number two, Awareness? Let's change our language. To change your life, to awaken your inner Superhero, you need to believe in yourself. I am so fortunate to have had the dad I had. He taught me that I could do anything. I can do anything boys can do, I can be anything I want to be, but also that just because I can do anything, I don't have to do everything. Thanks, Dad. I grew up with a belief system that allowed my inner Superhero to grow and not be stifled by limiting beliefs. This is not to say that I didn't hear negative things from some adults when I was a child, like my aunt telling me I had no talent. For years, that belief crippled me and kept me from even trying to write or create. How sad that so many of us let ourselves be defined by someone else's beliefs about us.

If you didn't have a Superhero dad as I did, and maybe you got negative messaging or lacked in positive role models when you were a child, all is not lost. To activate your Unstoppable Power, you first need to recognize your own limiting beliefs and then challenge yourself to discover where you learned them. Our beliefs about ourselves now are created by experiences in our past, but the past is the past. Any event that led to a negative belief was just an experience. Good or bad, they are all only experiences, and once they're over, they are over. We don't need to bring with us any baggage from the trip. Learn what that it's there to teach and move on. Being engaged in the present moment, being aware of our choices now, being willing to let go of the past, and forgiving, with kindness, ourselves, and everyone who helped create our limiting beliefs, opens us up to allow a myriad of possibilities into our lives.

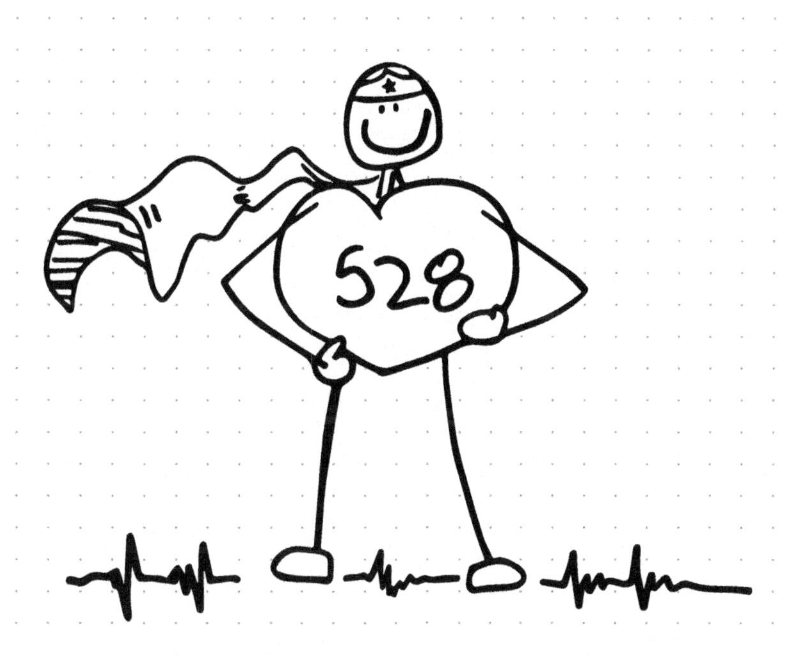
528

Always believe something wonderful is about to happen. Not to spoil the ending for you, but things are going to turn out alright. Think of your worst day, the absolute worst thing that has ever happened in your life. Guess what? You made it through. You're here, and things are okay. Examine your belief systems. From who, when, and where did you learn them? This awareness will empower you to change the beliefs you need to change to become your best self. Believe in yourself. Believe in your power.

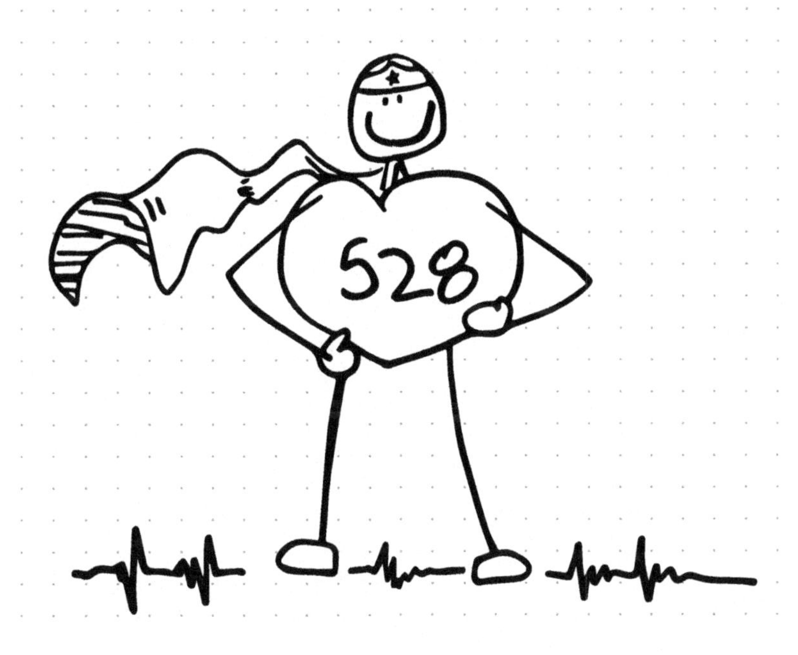
528

Exercise

The movement I teach for embodying a belief is a standing forward fold. This movement is an excellent stretch for your hamstrings and back. It is also known to be beneficial for alleviating stress, asthma, and high blood pressure. Now, by all means, if you have a back issue, or this causes any pain or discomfort, DON'T DO IT. That goes for all of the movements we're practicing. Listen to your body.

When I speak to audiences and tell them we're going to do a forward fold and touch our toes, invariably, many of them say, "I can't do that." That's an excellent example of a limiting belief. Stand tall with your feet hip-width apart and stretch your spine with your ears to the ceiling. Take a deep breath in, and as you exhale, slowly bend at the hips drawing your chest towards your thighs. Let your head and arms hang towards the floor. Staying relaxed, slowly move into the stretch until your fingertips reach your toes. Some people can place their palms on the floor comfortably. You can stay in the fold for up to a minute.

To release the fold, put your hands on your hips, keep your back flat, and inhale as you come back to standing. Did you touch your toes? If not, why not? If you said, "I can't touch my toes," your belief has created your reality. What if you said, "I can if I bend my knees"? The impossible has become possible through language and belief.

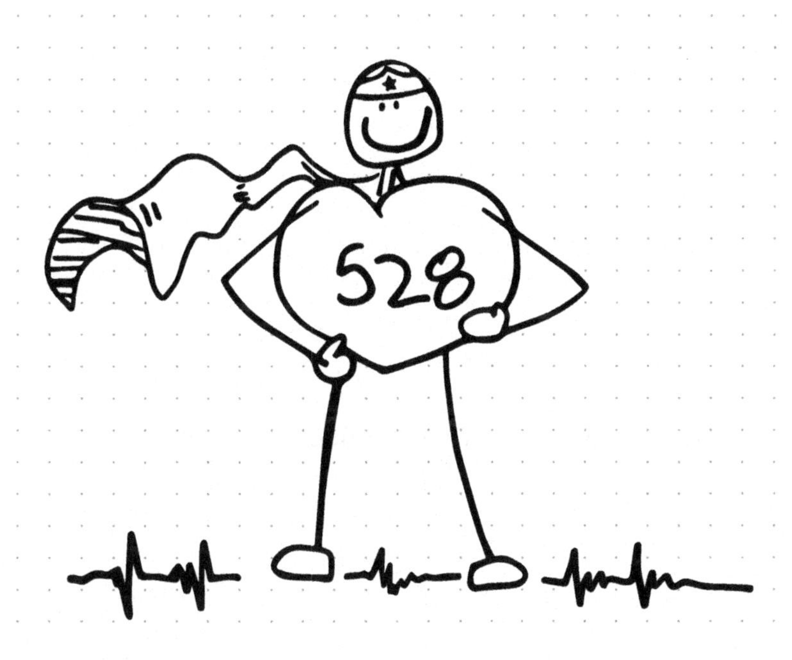
528

Belief I.Q.s

What do I believe about a higher power?

Where, when and who did this belief come from?

What do I believe about my worthiness? (Am I worthy of receiving love? All the good things coming into my life?)

Where, when and who did this belief come from?

What do I believe others believe about me?

Why?

Do I have a belief that may not fit me anymore?

And what is the belief I can replace it with?

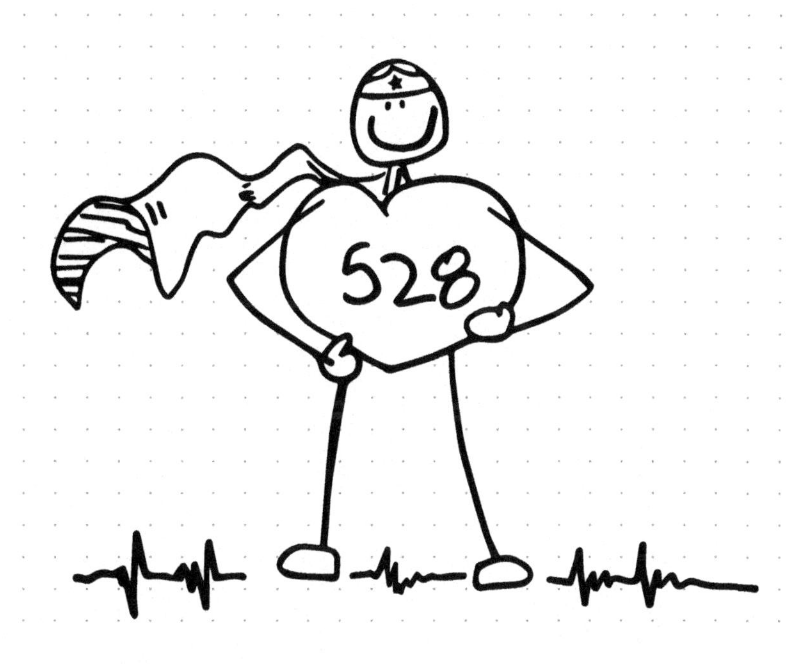
528

SUPERPOWER #8: LOVE

Be Love

Your power comes when you love without hesitation.

ROBIN O'BRIEN

Superpower #8: Love

Your strongest Superhero power is, without a doubt, Love. It is the overriding energy of the universe. I met Lois when I was sixteen-years-old. I answered an ad for a part-time job in a little corner convenience store not far from where I lived, and Lois owned that store. I was a bit afraid of her at first. She was a strong personality and didn't take any guff from anyone. I grew to respect and love her as a second mom. When she retired and sold the business, she moved to Florida, and I visited every year. One night, I got a phone call from her best friend. She was crying and told me that Lois had been diagnosed with stage 4 lung cancer. She was alone and very sick, and could I come? I was on a plane the next day. She had no family and no one to take care of her. I couldn't stay in Florida, so I convinced her to come home with me to Maine, where we started treatments for her at a cancer center near my home.

One morning I found her standing in the kitchen and crying. Through her tears, she told me she was sorry, sorry that I had to take care of her, sorry that I had to go all the way to Florida and get her, sorry that I was missing time from work to be with her. She was afraid I would put her in a nursing home. I said, "Lois, I didn't bring you all the way from Florida to put you in a nursing home. Besides, if the tables were turned, would you do the same thing for me?" Without hesitation, she said, "a million times over." That's the kind of love I'm talking about. Be willing to love unconditionally without hesitation.

Remember Superpower number two, Awareness? We learned to be aware of energy. 528hz is an energy frequency. It's the frequency that scientists have determined is the frequency of love. It's the frequency that our cells resonate when we are feeling love. It's the frequency of the internal energy that we are putting out into the world that others can feel when they are in our presence. I call it GLOWing, Giving Love Out to the World.

We've all met people that are exuding positivity and love, and we've met people who resonate with a harmful, pessimistic, angry kind of energy. You can feel it when they enter a room. They are like energy vampires and seem to create a vacuum that can sometimes make you feel like your breath is being sucked out of you. We know that like attracts like when it comes to energy. Entrainment is when our internal rhythms (frequency) will slow down or speed up to meet a stronger external rhythm. When I'm feeling anger, you feel it, and it starts to bring you down. If I'm feeling love, you feel it too, and your energy rises to entrain (or match) that frequency.

What we need to do is raise our frequency to a higher level of love. That's the secret to becoming A Superhero You. If we get down to basics, this is it. The Superpower above all powers. LOVE. Understand that the power is not to "be more loving." It's to BE LOVE. You need to GLOW. Give love out to the world, unconditionally, without hesitation. How do we do that? An easy way to raise your vibration to a more loving place is to think of something, someone, someplace, that makes you feel love. It makes you happy, smile, feel relaxed, and feel love. For me, it's Winston, my little rescue dog. He's a Shih-Tzu-Yorkie mix. When I think of him, I can't be upset or angry or depressed. Thinking of him brings to mind unconditional love. For some people, it's a pet, or a child, or maybe an event or a place, anything that makes you feel that kind of love.

528

Exercise

Try this. Close your eyes, take a few deep, opening breaths, and relax, maybe a cycle of box breaths. Now bring to mind someone, someplace, or something that makes you feel love. See it and feel it. Your vibration will rise, and so will the frequency of those around you. Back to basics. Love yourself and love one another unconditionally.

Glow, baby, and we're all Superheroes.

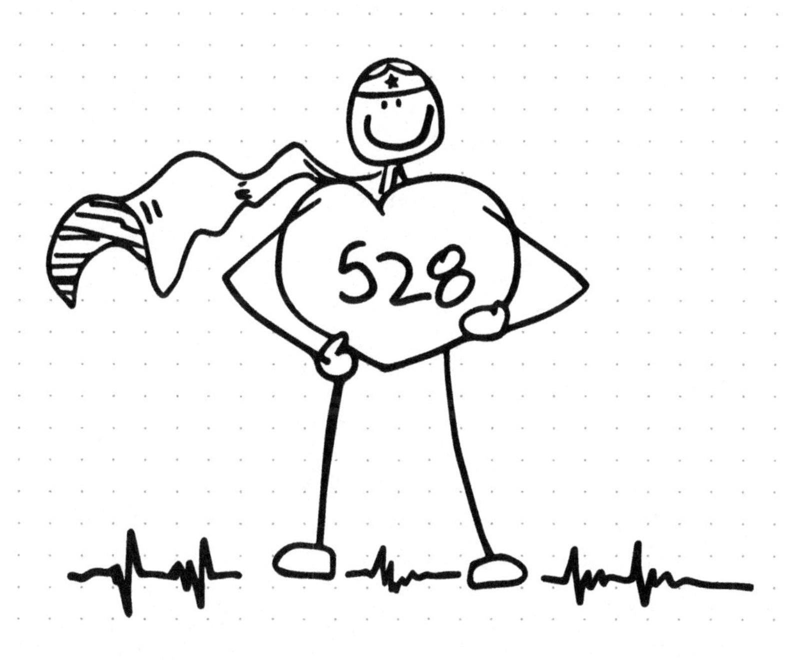
528

Love I.Q.s

Am I feeling love energy today? Y / N

How specifically will I raise my vibrations today so that others will feel it? (turn on that GLOW!)

Who in my life needs more love today?

How will I bring/send them love?

Do I need to feel more love from others?

Who will I ask for love? (we're so afraid to ask for what we need, and love is a basic need. Ask!)

How did it make me feel to ask?

And to receive?

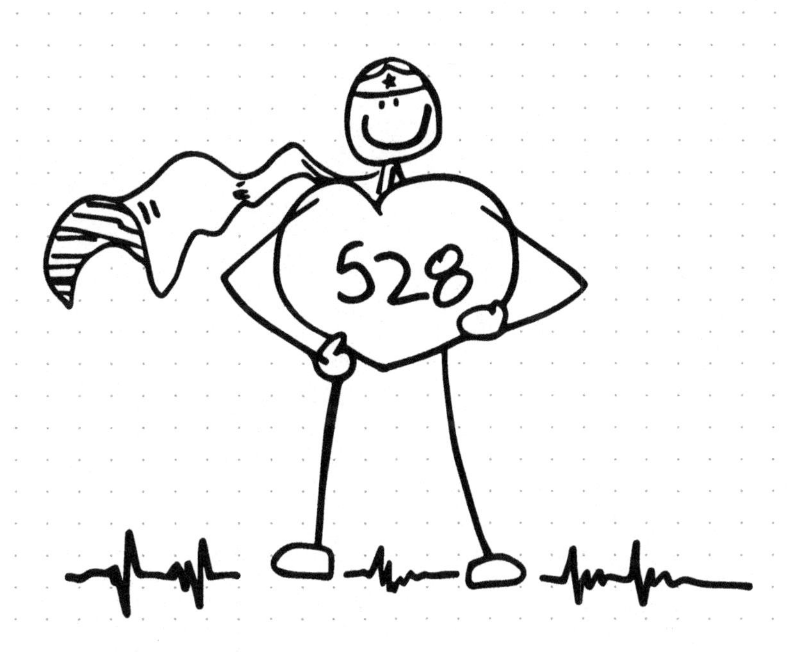
528

Troubleshooting Questions

If you find yourself in a difficult situation where you're feeling less than powerful, using the following questions as a quick checklist will help. They are the questions I ask myself when I'm stuck, need guidance, or need to make an important choice.

Am I grounded around this situation? Am I focused and engaged?

Am I aware of the energy I bring to this situation? Am I staying positive with my language and aware of the choices I have?

Am I willing to make the decisions that best serve me without guilt?

Am I open to different ideas and possibilities, listening and hearing other opinions? Have I opened up to signs that are affirming?

Am I confident in my abilities?

Am I being kind to myself, and to others, especially when stressed about a problem?

Do I believe that this will turn out the way I intend? When it's supposed to? Or do I have limiting beliefs that are hindering me?

Am I GLOWing? Am I coming from a place of love and giving love in this situation?

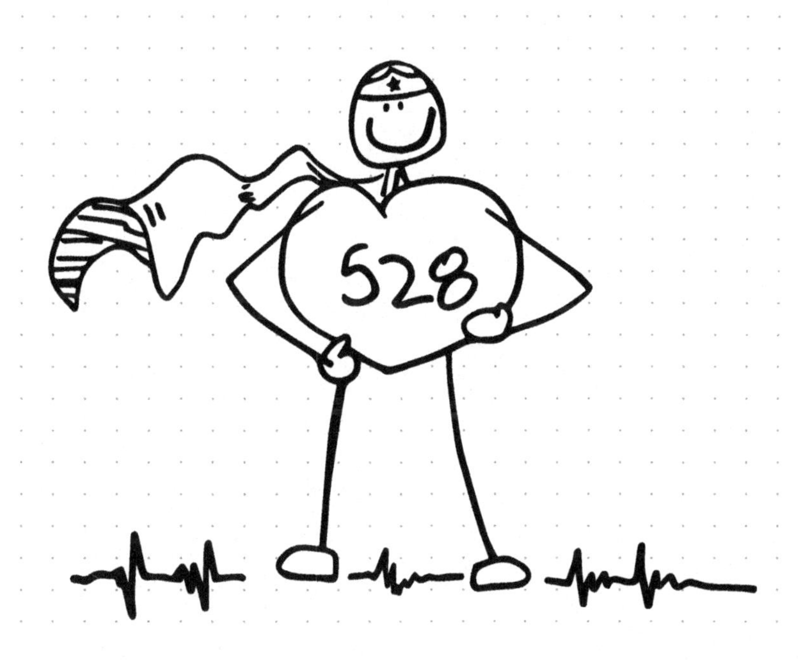
528

A Superhero You

Congratulations! You've done the work, you've asked the introspective questions of yourself, and you've remembered the Superpowers that will dissolve what's been holding you back from being A Superhero You. Use what you've learned about yourself to move and grow forward. My wish for you is that you GLOW in all that you do. If you will, your impact will expand in immeasurable ways. GLOWing together, we can change the world, one Superhero at a time.

With much Love,
Barb

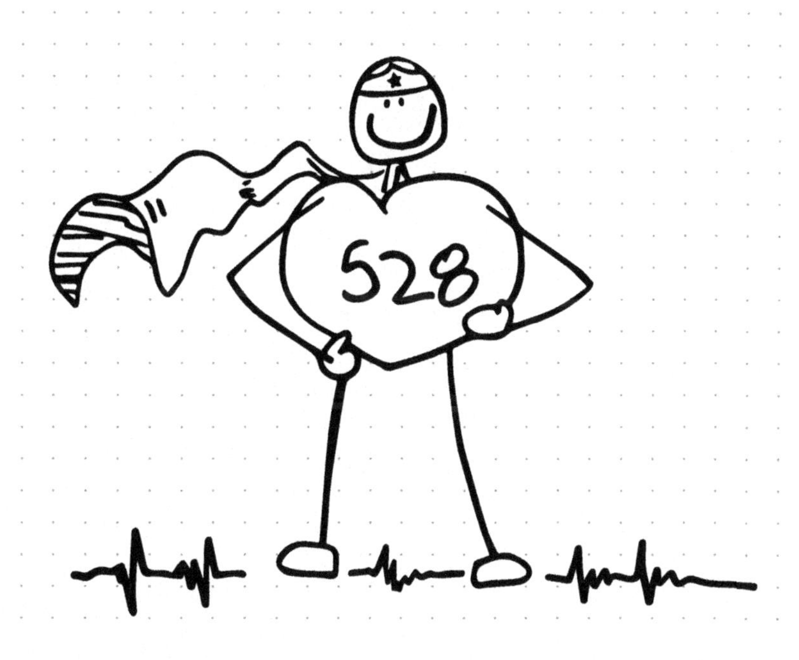
528

A Superhero You Checklist

To help you to incorporate these powers in your daily life, I've created A Superhero You Checklist. It is available for you to download and print at www.BarbaraAnneCookson/ASYChecklist

I use this checklist every day so I've laminated mine to reuse. It's a great way to spend a few minutes in the morning to create a super day. I've included easy instructions that will help you to maximize your productivity as well. I'd love to hear from you about how this workbook has helped you activate A Superhero You. Contact me at www.BarbaraAnneCookson.com

Made in the USA
Middletown, DE
21 November 2019